YE GODS—

I0134714

by

ED WILLOCK

Illustrated by the Author

Catholic Authors Press
Hartford, 2006

Ye Gods consists of articles that originally appeared in The Torch, and were collected in this edition in 1948 by Sheed & Ward.

ISBN: 0-9776168-7-8

Printed in the United States of America

Catholic Authors Press
www.CatholicAuthors.org

*Dedicated to My
Wife, Dorothy*

INTRODUCTION

THERE is an observation generally held to be true, today, which I think is untrue. It is claimed that our contemporary pagans in America are not religious, that they are practical, hard-headed, and believe only what they see. My observations are to the contrary. The moderns are quite religious about the things that require hard-headed practicality, and they are hard-headedly agnostic about the things that should evoke religious reverence. They approach a bank or a stock report with the most reverent awe, and yet turn a calculating eye upon the Church and the priesthood. They won't be taken in by the gospels, but they will be taken in by the racing-form. They stand aghast at the superstition of Quebec peasants who manifest their faith in frugal homes and majestic cathedrals. They accept with religious docility the fact that New Yorkers abide in cement boxes and erect towering monuments to the gods of commerce from which

sacrificial victims leap to their death with monoto-
nous regularity. Their hard heads cannot fathom
the mystery of young men and women giving their
lives to God behind cloistered walls, yet they incant
litanies of economic mysteries in defense of the
practice of chaining men to factory assembly lines,
or women to office typewriters.

They scorn the sentimentalists who ask another
dime per hour for the men who mine their coal, and
then proceed to deluge home-run hitters with gold
beyond the dream of ancient kings. In defense of
every political and economic move they marshal
a series of platitudes which parallel in logic and
clarity the prayers of a Fiji Island witch doctor to
the goddess of fertility.

There is no way of debating the rationality of
these peculiar customs. The norms of the modern
mystics are not based upon a perverted philosophy
but upon an elaborate mythology. In every argument with them the Christian is asked to offer incense before some strange fabricated idol. If one
inquires just a little beneath the pragmatic explanation the modern pagan gives, one encounters

a mystery. It is a mystery more like a mirage than a miracle. It is a belief not beyond reason, such as that of the Christian mystic, but a belief that has nothing to do with reason at all. Their ultimate faith is an idolatry of creatures unhampered by authoritative revelation, and they cling to it with the persistency of religious fanatics.

In this they are unlike the Christian mystics, who always display a breath-taking matter-of-factness about things that are just a matter of fact. Saint Francis of Assisi gloried in the laws of nature and playfully gave personalities to the sun and the stars. He would never have enshrined these phenomena or endowed them with the infallibility that a Wall Street broker attributes to his cherished law of supply and demand. The Christian description of an angel is more precise than a modern economist's definition of a price curve. The medieval mystic had a reasonable explanation of why hell is overpopulated, but a modern sociologist's excuse for the overpopulation of New York City is pure mysticism. The ancient mystics catalogued human virtues with the quiet accuracy of a physicist counting atoms. An editorial in a popular weekly written in praise of free-enterprise is as inaccurate and exaggerated as a swain's description of his beloved.

The ancient saint and the modern pagan have this in common: they are both mystics. The difference between them is that the saint is mystical about mysteries and reasonable about facts; the pagan is ignorant about mysteries and mystical about facts. The saint tries to see what *is there* but cannot be seen; the neo-pagan sees something that *isn't there at all.*

In this book I have catalogued some of these modern mysticisms. You will not find here any of the strange foreign ideologies to which our politicians so frequently allude. These are America's household gods. These are the myths upon which our social norms are based. These are the spirits that inform the institutions of Wall Street and of Main Street. Formal introductions are unnecessary.

CONTENTS

CONTENTS

BELIEVING IN ONESELF

BELIEVING IN ONESELF

THE most worthy activity of the human person is contemplation. Saint Thomas tells us that all of man's activity has as its end the securing of the necessary leisure for contemplation. (It is noteworthy, incidentally, that none of our manufacturers of leisure-creating devices has thus far used this argument as a selling-point.)

The gentleman in the illustration is indulging in the modern substitute for that activity recommended so highly by the Angelic Doctor. The incense of virile masculinity rises solemnly from his cigar. His nerveless fingers have let fall that Bible of hard facts and progress: *The Times*. Effortlessly his imagination embraces the deity it has sired. On the screen of his closed eyelids appears that magnificent phenomenon, a god made to the image and likeness of man. The hand of the deity is raised in a beneficent sign of victory, and the divine lips plagiarize convincingly, "In this sign thou shalt conquer."

Communion between shadow and substance becomes complete. The consummating act of love is achieved: the love of a man for his *ego*. Penitently he confesses those few instances of disloyalty when his faith in himself had faltered, those rash moments when the tenets of "How to Win Friends and Influence People" had been defied. All of his relationships he carefully re-orients, evaluating them in terms of their contribution to his importance:

"Did it pay to be lenient with his debtors?"

"Was he giving enough to his family so that they might worthily reflect his importance?"

"Would going to church on Sunday do *him* any good?"

"Had he been quick in the defense of all *his* rights?"

"Had he taken advantage of all the deductions on his income tax?"

"Was he being fair to himself?"

"Was he getting the most out of life?"

Thus, we see unfolded the strange liturgy common to the modern mystic: the man who *believes* in himself.

If believing in oneself were an erroneous philosophy, it might be more easily corrected. A false philosophy is an attempt at logic which falls short, and to set it aright we need only find the break in the logical chain and mend it. Believing in oneself is a false religion. It is the acceptance of a testimony of which the person is at one and the same time the god, the prophet, and the disciple. It is a religion so exclusive that it could not tolerate more than one saint.

There is a Christian idea of which this cult is a caricature. Our Lord tells us "The Kingdom of Heaven is within you." By this is meant that our citizenship in Christ's Kingdom is not a matter of outward glory, but of inner disposition. Our bond with the Kingdom is an invisible quality of spirit rather than an outward display of manners. The mark of our birthright is upon our hearts. There may be no reference to it on our social security card, or in the social register.

Every man is aware of this inner greatness either as an actuality or a potentiality. The mystic who believes in himself knows it only in the breach. He contemplates a capacity awesome in its emptiness. Nowhere through the five windows of his senses can he see any delight that could assuage the intensity of his desire. He cherishes this emptiness of heart much as a childless wife enshrines an empty cradle. His spiritual geography is accurate. He retires to his own heart, just as the shepherd and wise man entered the stable at Bethelem hoping that the Savior would be there. Because of his spiritual astigmatism, however, the modern mystic pays tribute to the ass rather than to the Infant King.

The cult of those who believe in themselves would soon become extinct if those who had already found their Savior bore witness in word and deed to the place and nature of His Presence.

COUNTING NOSES

COUNTING NOSES

IN OUR DAY it has become frightfully important to know how many people are doing what. Organized bodies of men are kept busy with adding machines estimating such facts as: how many married persons between the ages of twenty-five and thirty wish they weren't; how many people drive cars; how many people the people who drive cars run over, and so on. Counting noses has become a business: quite a profitable business, judging by the awed respect extended to the Gallup and Hooper polls. It was a mysticism, however, long before it was a business.

Business men know that the best way to make a product popular is to say that it is popular. Politicians know that one way to get votes is to state emphatically that everyone is going to vote for them. This is a situation peculiar to modern society. At other times in history, and in other places in the world, men would say: "What difference does it make how many people do a thing? What conceivable relation is there between what people do and the question of whether it is the *right* thing to do? Ten million people drink tea. So what? I prefer goat's milk!" This sort of reasoning only exists where the mysticism of counting noses is unknown. This stubborn individualism is in direct violation of the modern article of faith: "The majority is always right."

History attests to the fact that the majority is seldom right. The rare chance that the majority might be right decreases in inverse proportion to the number of people who expect it to happen. This reduces the chance of its happening today to zero. The mystical belief that counting noses is a way to determine the virtuousness or judiciousness of a habit, is the one guarantee that the majority will inevitably and constantly be *wrong*.

There is more than one reason why the unreasonable belief in majority righteousness exists. I will give three:

FIRST: Ours is a materialistic society. Materialists have no truck with quality because quality is a *spiritual* thing. You can neither see it nor price it. The materialist can, however, understand quantity. To his obtuse mind, the more there is of a thing, the better it is. Thus he attributes virtue to majority opinion simply because there are more ballots counted.

SECOND: In modern overcrowded cities the easiest *physical* thing to do is follow the crowd. We all become accustomed to lining-up one behind the other as passengers for vehicles, customers for groceries, or penitents for Confession. Most of the daily work that we do can best be done by watching the girl or fellow beside us. In other words, we get along best by going with the crowd. This becomes habitual. After awhile it is difficult to think for ourselves, invent new methods, or make new choices. Thus we come to feel that following the crowd is the *right* thing to do.

THIRD: The desire to conform today has reached the proportions of a chronic panic. Everyone is afraid that *his* nose is the one that will not be counted. "Everyone in the neighborhood will have television but *me!*" "All of the children on Easter

Sunday will be well dressed but *mine!*" Behind it all is a horror of being conspicuous.

The thing we mustn't forget is that the most important things that happen to us, happen to us apart from the crowd, such as birth and Baptism, death and Judgment. We should be preparing for these last things by being ourselves even to the point of being conspicuous. Remember how conspicuous the Man was Who hung on a cross, silhouetted against a troubled sky. Then remember the crowd who stood below Him with up-turned noses.

OMNI-SCIENCE

OMNI-SCIENCE

HIROSHIMA was the marriage feast at Cana for the omni-scientist. It was his first public miracle. Thus began his public life. The day was premature perhaps, but could he refuse the motherly request of political expediency? Had he ever refused her anything?

In fulfillment of the prophecies of H. G. Wells and Buck Rogers the new messiah has arrived. He stands transfigured between the two prophets of the old law, War and Commerce, prophets of a law which he comes not to destroy but to fulfill.

A member of the cloth (the men in white), in a recent encyclical addressed to the laity, predicted that when mankind becomes aware of the tremendous significance of atomic power and its portents for the future, we shall date our calendars A.B. (after the bomb) rather than A.D. (anno Domini). This is a statement more religious than scientific in its implications. We are called to accept a new savior.

Pale young men with brief cases climb the steps of our cathedrals of science and work in silent dedication under fluorescent lamps. Eager young women have found a more compelling vocation among the microbes than had been their lot among the shoppers and the busy business men. There is a new zest in the air mingled with the fumes of high octane, formaldehyde, and D.D.T. The answers to the earth's riddles are calmly transcribed from complex dials. The uplift of the working classes has become for the physicist a question of levitation, for the psychiatrist a question of levity, and for the physician a question of transfusion and vitamins.

Common gossip quivers to the terms of the new liturgy; radar, super-sonic, atomic fission, psychosomatic, electronic, RH negative, and these are treated with the same reverent lack of understanding formerly reserved for the Nicene Creed.

Circumstantial evidence, along with the willingness of the omni-scientist to play the part, has pushed the scientist into a role which stands part way between that of a witch doctor and a priest. When men put a ceiling on speculation, shutting out anything that couldn't be seen, smelled, tasted or touched, they automatically appointed the scientist king of the roost. Every day, however, the scientist is bumping his head against this ceiling. His prying curiosity is forever leading him into areas beyond his ken. His microscope and butterfly net fail to capture these nebulous things called life, and force, and happiness, and love. The very unwillingness of the omni-scientist to admit that these things are beyond him, confirms the opinion of the reader of the Sunday supplement that he *knows* but won't tell. The fraud is perpetuated by periodic statements to the press designed to mystify rather than clarify. Certain feats of legerdemain performed with tsetse flys or the sperm of an Alpine goat create the impression in the imaginations of the gullible that the scientist is a kind of god whom even the winds and the waves obey.

As a consequence of this new mysticism the scientist is employed by corporations and by governments to unloose any kind of monster on society. To stay his hand would be presumption. To question his right is blasphemy. He is the high-priest of the great god Matter, and after all, nothing matters but matter.

ACCENTUATING THE POSITIVE

ACCENTUATING THE
POSITIVE

THE conspiracy against the Faith as it goes on in every age is not as chaotic or disordered an attack as we would like to suppose. There is a real and powerful intellect weaving together the threads of sin and temptation into a unified pattern. The mind behind this conspiracy is one worth respecting, for it is that of Lucifer, the Light-Bearer. Satan has his temples and they are built of the same kind of brick as the temples of Christ. His plan of campaign proceeds in a logical fashion from cause to effect. This is so true that when we do come upon one of his masterpieces, whether it be a man, a faith, or a technique of action, we are dazzled by its beauty, its undeniable logic, its genius of plan and execution. Just so that we might overlook this orderliness in the house of sin, and thus underestimate the enemy, Satan has presented us with another mysticism which I choose to call accentuating the positive.

The mentality bred by this mysticism can only see things as either good or indifferent. It refuses to admit the reality of Evil. It discounts the evidence of an active power for Evil in the world. The existence of Hell or of the Devil it regards as either doubtful or, at least, inconsequential. As a result, this mentality hides from the responsibility of reform by refusing to listen to any adverse criticism of things as they are. It is reluctant to examine parts of its own conscience, with the same false delicacy that prompts a housewife to pass by a particularly dark and dirty corner of the attic. Yet it might be in that particular corner that vermin are breeding which will spread their foulness throughout those parts of the house which are daily cleaned and polished. A person thus afflicted will delight in all of God's nice things. She will glory in the angelic beauty of an infant's smile, but will shrink from changing its diaper. He will rave about the cuisine and services in a modern restaurant but not inquire into the nasty conditions that prompt the unionist to picket outside the entrance. This mysticism will focus itself upon the gay attractiveness of the sinner, the social charm of the usurer, the adventurous daring of the thief, the bluff good nature of the grafter, the smooth wit of the agnostic, but will carefully filter out the viciousness that accompanies these virtues.

This attitude is one of the greatest obstacles to any kind of reform. A person must become convinced that something is bad before he makes an attempt to correct it. Not every man who cries out against injustice is a malcontent. There are poets in every age who say that their times are decadent, but there are times when the poet is right. There are prophets in every age who prophesy a day of reckoning, and days of reckoning have not always failed to come. The confessor who warns one that a vice must be curbed is not being negative. A doctor who tells one his appendix must be removed is not just a pessimist. A social reformer who says the present order must go may not be a neurotic. A plumber who says the boiler will burst might not merely be looking for business. There is always the chance that an alarmist does see something to get alarmed about.

There are times when it is difficult to be positive. There are Good Fridays to be endured; there are foods to be left uneaten; there are wounds that must be inflicted; there is death to be faced. Evil is not everything, but it is something. It is a dragon all foul and evil, whose presence we must admit before we can lift our lance to shoulder. We must first see where Christ is *not* before we can bring Him there.

ROMANCE

ROMANCE

ST. TERESA called the imagination "the fool of the household." When the modern man forsook God, he forsook reality. A mind without the discipline of the Holy Ghost becomes a playground for the mad antics of the imagination. Stepping through that looking-glass which had once reflected a true image, the modern man has wandered into the garden and down the rabbit's hole. As a result, the borderline between fiction and fact is the most bitterly contested and most poorly defined boundary of modern history.

Let us stroll down Main Street and breathe the fog of enchantment as it rolls in from the Sea of Romance. Over there is a gaily lighted marquee, the Temple of Torpor. Inside men are sitting in silence, backs turned to the world, preoccupied with the activity of shadows cast upon a wall. Watch Mr. Binkle in the third row. See him as he walks between the lines of plumed centurians.

27

Slowly he climbs the marble steps to stand scowling before Cleopatra. Tomorrow, until the spell is over, he will be Claude Rains among his hardware. He will wonder, "Why must romance flee at fifty?" By Mrs. Binkle he will be misunderstood.

Across the street, in that small white house, live the Wattles. Mrs. Wattles, sitting alone, looks out into the darkness. This evening at dinner Mr. Wattles had had "that strange look of not being sure." Perhaps for her, just as for Chichi (of "Life Can Be Peachy"), this is "the end." Perhaps "the wells of love have dried as a rose lies crushed without sweetness." Ten more episodes of "Chichi" and the Wattles will wend their individual ways to the law courts. Mrs. Wattles plans (if it does happen) to retain "a dramatic silence, her blue eyes dry, her face without color save for the bold despair of her crimson mouth."

Young Joe Carr, escorting Martha Kemp, alights from a cab. Laughing, they enter the Saucy Goose night club. It is the girl's first fling at life. Her mother had been slow with her consent, but then, had not the heroine of her latest novel said, "Youth without romance is ashes"? Joe is leaving for camp tomorrow. His speech awaits the opportune moment: "Is it a sin to love as we love? Would it not be a greater sin against love to deny it?"

Here is the Town Hall. Representative Higgins is concluding a bitter tirade against the natives of Moscow, Madrid, and Belgrade, places the existence of which he knows only by hearsay. All this romantic rot, while the local garbage, the local firetraps, and the local graft go uncollected, uninspected, and uncorrected.

At the end of the block is a church unoccupied except for the Reality of Realities. Under the guise of bread Christ lives in the midst of His people. From Him proceeds the merciful gift of imagination. Through its magic eye we sense the Invisible. With this faculty we anticipate the Vision as yet unseen. It is not given us that we might cut our heaven from cardboard, paint it, sprinkle it with perfume, and call it LIFE.

VARIETY

VARIETY

VARIETY is the spice of life. It is the kind of spice being used today to make an otherwise tasteless mess of pottage palatable. Variety is the haystack in which the precious needle of salvation is so difficult to find. Variety is one of the most subtle of the new mysticisms.

The grandest gesture a man can make is to make a choice. On this gesture depends his temporal well-being, his vocation, and his eternal life. "Do you renounce the devil in all his works and pomps?" I DO. "Do you take this woman as your lawful wedded wife?" I DO. "Are you sorry for your sins?" I AM.

In answering such questions as these, man (through the infinite mercy of God) decides his temporal and eternal destiny. But, there are other questions: "Will you have the special dinner with french fries, mashed, home fries, baked, or boiled potatoes?" "Will I wear the brown skirt and white

33

blouse with my sport shoes, or the green dress with the yellow jacket and my high heels?" "Will we go to the Kozy Korner for dinner and then see Humphrey Brogan in 'Gentlemen are Bums,' or will we see Abigail Squash in 'Life With My Father-in-law,' and *then* go to The Pelican Club for the floor show?" "Will I read some historical fiction by Kenneth Roberts, or some fictional history by Van Loon, or will I just stand here all day and read the titles?"

Not only are the first group important questions, and the second group indifferent, but also, the first group are leading questions, and the second group terminal questions. When you say, "I do take this woman!" you are really starting something, but when you arise and trumpet to the world your singular devotion to french-fried potatoes, you have nothing more to do than eat them and pay the check. A grand and noble choice, such as admitting your sins, sets you on a path lined with innumerable minor choices, all related to your first decision. After you have seen Humphrey Brogan, all you have left is a headache.

A man surrounded by a variety of desirable goods finds it difficult to live up to the major decisions of his life. He is tempted in either of two directions. He may be led down innumerable blind alleys of frustrated desires or indifferent decisions. For instance, he may spend many of his hours deciding which hat, which razor, which ball-game, which flavor, which novel, or which cigarette. His other temptation will be to lapse into day-dreams, finding delight in imagined experiences of endless variety, while failing to make the decisions in his real affairs which duty requires. The person who gets that way is a convert to the mysticism of variety.

In an age when a moral sense set certain limits both to men's possessions and to men's desires to acquire them, it was easier for a man to set his mind to the things that matter. Today, no such limits are drawn. All of us fall prey to the persuasions of any merchant who can afford to advertise. Without a conscious effort on our part, we are made aware of the existence of fifty-seven varieties of soup, while it is only with considerable effort that we can recall or discover if the gifts of the Holy Ghost are six or seven.

Until the times change, and they will, there is no escaping the mysticism of Variety other than the practice of voluntary poverty. We must let the Holy Ghost set our course, and then steer clear of the reefs of desirable possessions. We will find that the goods we require for the practice of virtue and the accomplishment of our vocation are both specific and singular, not various and multiple. As we strip for Catholic Action we will be amazed at how many things we *don't* need. We will discover that no one ever possesses a variety of goods, they are only possessed *by* them.

EFFICIENCY

E. WILLOCK

EFFICIENCY

EFFICIENCY is the business of getting a thing done (no matter what it is) in the shortest possible time and with a minimum expenditure of effort and money. It is considered among the primary virtues today. If we were to stop for a moment, and instead of taking the virtue for granted, look at it objectively, we would find that it has very little to recommend it as an addition to traditional human virtues As far as doing a thing rapidly is concerned, there are times when speed is of the essence, as for instance in putting out a fire, or applying a tourniquet. Within reason, speed in traveling has something to be said for it. Common experience, however, affords ample evidence that our moderns do not simply ask for efficiency in matters of travel or first aid. You would have to pause for a moment to think of anything that our contemporaries prefer to have accomplished *slowly*.

Mary Jane is praised as a good typist because she

can beat out 125 words a minute on her Under-
wood. P. J. Swiven is lauded as a competent executive because he can clean up his mail, dictate his
correspondence, and issue directives, all before
noon, thus leaving his afternoon free for golf.
Julius Blerp has just received a medal for crating
his millionth egg without ever breaking a shell.
Mrs. Epson gets her housework done by eleven,
leaving time every day for movies, bridge and club
meetings. Now, simply on the basis of these facts,
can we find anything particularly virtuous in these
accomplishments?

The intimation is that there is virtue in typing
125 words a minute regardless of whether they are
words of scorn, blackmail, devotion, hypocrisy, or
theology. The fact of whether Mary Jane is aware of
what she is typing or not, is not so much as considered. Yet, before we can determine the morality of her acts, these are the facts that we must
know.

P. J. Swiven may have turned down a request for
funds from a starving missionary, or passed the
buck to ten overworked secretaries. All we know is

that he did it with dispatch at a saving of time and money.

Were Julius Blerp's eggs overpriced or overripe? Did he crate them for the honor and glory of God? We don't know, but he did it efficiently. What did Mrs. Epson do with the time she saved? Was the common good served by her afternoon activities? Perhaps not, but then, we are forgetting: efficiency has been made an end in itself!

This much is pretty obvious: efficiency has nothing to do with morality, and nothing to do with art. When you have said that, you can go right on to say that it has nothing to do with human virtue. Removing morality or art from the consideration of human acts leaves no alternative but to judge them in terms of mechanical competence. In other words, efficiency is a mechanical virtue. To say a man is efficient is to say that he is a very good machine.

There are two rather good reasons why efficiency is considered to be a virtue in this particular year of Our Lord. The first and most obvious reason is that men have forgotten that this *is* a year of Our Lord. If they had not forgotten that all-important fact, they would not have devised a social system in which men are praised for being machines. When it is no longer considered important to do a morally good job, or an esthetically good job, the only norm left is to do a mechanically good job. If you can't work enthusiastically, you can still work rapidly. Though you can't increase the quality of the product, you can decrease its cost of production.

The second reason for efficiency being considered a virtue is that it is a caricature of skill. It is a machine acting like a man. You have heard it said of some particular machine, "It's almost human." The griddlecake maker in the bakery window is doing a job that seems almost human. He exhibits the same economy of effort and the same graceful ease as a concert pianist. But there the resemblance ends. The concert pianist has highly developed intellectual virtues for which his nimble fingers are merely the instruments. The griddlecake maker is flipping this ten thousandth cake purely automatically. His dexterity is enhanced by the fact that his mind is elsewhere. He is a machine giving a fairly good imitation of a man.

Efficiency will be considered a virtue as long as it is profitable to reduce men to the level of automatons. In the meantime the Faith stands very much in need of saints, preferably inefficient ones like the Curé d'Ars.

GLAMOUR

GLAMOUR

THE most normal thing in the world is for men and women to be interested in one another. Everyone is happy when this interest crystallizes in the form of a vocation. Until that happy state is achieved there is a certain amount of necessary trial and error. This period of shopping for a mate is usually, and very excusably, attended by the contestants' making themselves attractive to one another. The mysticism of glamour has something to do with the pluming and preening of the ladies. As a means to the end of matrimony it is, to say the least, peculiar. The atmosphere created with pads and paint and perfume has a pseudo-olympian flavor about it, as though the person being ornamented were no mere woman but rather a goddess. It would seem to the disinterested observer, that glamour is a technique for attracting worshippers rather than lovers.

The girl next door just received her diploma from high school the other day. This afternoon you saw emerging from her doorway a creature combining the more formidable features of Cleopatra and Lady Macbeth. When you had overcome the first emotion of reverent awe to the extent of lifting your eyes to the beatific face, you recognized little Agnes. The shoemaker, hairdresser, and milliner had, by taking thought, added a few cubits to her stature. The tailor had extended her horizontally with the aid of shoulder pads. Her very spaciousness, the amount of vertical and horizontal area she covered, would make any man feel inferior unless he were riding a horse.

The idea for this get-up didn't originate with Agnes. A number of magazines supply the cant and ritual for those women who make a fetish of this kind of garb. The descriptive language common to these publications resembles in a crude way, the psalms of David. For example, here are a few choice bits:

YOU are fluid, you are a changing thing, you are never finished, you are always becoming,—You *can* gain new power over yourself!—Picture yourself as you *want* to look! (A description of a shoe)

Party pretty, yet classic. The magic pump that will dress you up and down, and is fashioned with *his* heart in mind.—Soon you'll find yourself smiling in the mirror at a new *YOU* . . . prettier than you ever, in your wildest dreams, thought possible.

Poor Agnes! She's never finished, always becoming. It sounds rather tedious.

The mysticism of glamour is something distinct from the process of a girl's gilding her native beauty with the idea of attracting a husband. A judicious arrangement of clothes and cosmetics can bring innate feminine virtue out from under a bushel so that it may shine before the otherwise non-discerning male. The glamour girl, if that is her intention, is missing the target by a mile. Glamour doesn't attract, it alarms. The glamour girl isn't a sight to behold, she's just a sight. The glamour girl seems to be looking for a pedestal and a vigil light.

The aura of glamour is a base caricature of the aura of sanctity. In Christian societies, women shared the dignity of Mary, their mother. This dignity was reflected in their style of dress and ornament. In our times, however, it is not Mary but the woman of easy virtue who has been reflected in the feminine styles. The fashions have not spoken of modesty or motherhood, but rather of the boudoir and the affair.

The mysticism of glamour is a vain and pitiful attempt to achieve the appearance of invincible virtue and aloofness which naturally exudes from the daughter of Mary. It is an unconscious nostalgia for the quiet dignity which envelopes a Christian Virgin, Nun *or* Mother.

The problem posed by the new mysticism of glamour is one that can best be answered by Catholic women. It should not be too hard to design women's clothes and styles which would be both contemporary and Christian. Purity, modesty, and gentleness can be expressed in costume and manner so as to capture the attention of any man who loves Our Lady. It is sad that such lovable and attractive virtues are frequently hidden beneath the grotesque trappings of "the glamour girl."

HEALTH

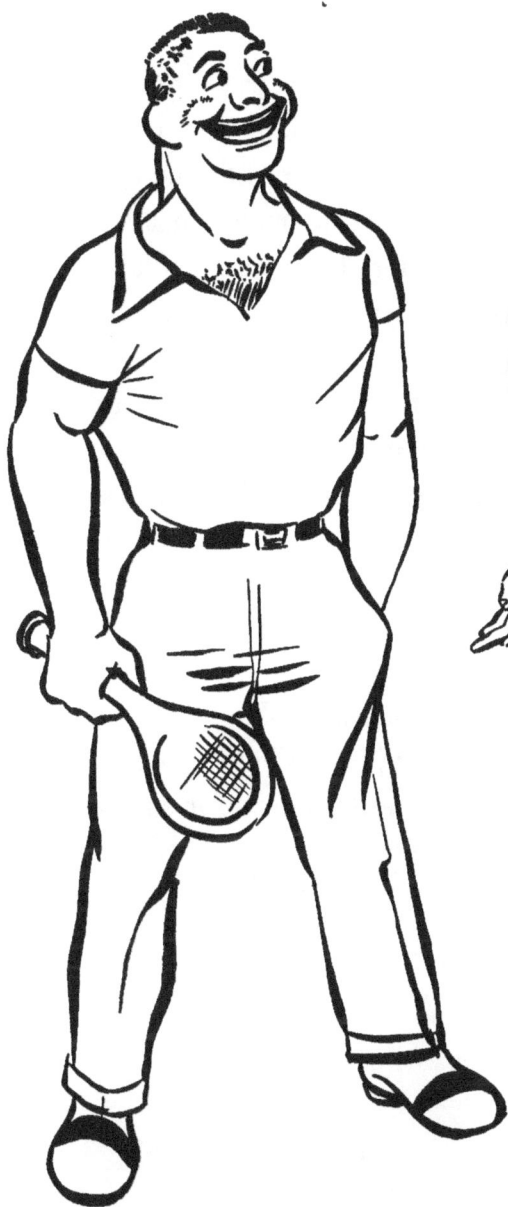

HEALTH

IT IS pretty obvious that people think too much about their health these days. Many people worry themselves sick about it. A person with one foot in the grave may excusably be interested in keeping the other foot from slipping. But today we find people in perfect health worrying about (of all things) their health!

There are two general types of health-misers. The first is forever taking inventory of his large muscles, his excellent vision, her brilliance of teeth, her wave of hair, or his propensity for always feeling fit as a fiddle. The other health-miser is that melancholic creature who tours the subterranean passages of his innards, jotting notes on each bolt or fly-wheel not functioning as it should.

On the one hand we find Jane Vital throwing her weight about the beaches, gluttonous for sunshine and glow, leaving the mere matters of work and labor to her elderly, rheumatic ma and pa. On the other hand, we have Mrs. Bromide spending the best years of her life nursing an imaginary cancer, while her husband develops ulcers for lack of decently prepared meals, and her children are educated on the inner workings of mother, instead of the inner Life of the Holy Spirit.

I call this undue interest in bodily health a mysticism because it is not based upon reason, but upon a faith. It proceeds from some strange belief that health is to be fostered, served, and adored, as an end in itself.

A man is comparable to a castle, or, better still, to a temple. Many things go on in this temple, but the main thing is that God is worshipped there. In this temple man is a priest. His work as a priest is to offer sacrifice. The health maniac, instead of being a priest of the temple, prefers to be the janitor. His days are spent among the pipes and fuel bins, or polishing the exterior brasses. He putters around the temple busy with matters of heat, light or drainage. All of this is done to the exclusion of that act which gives all other acts their meaning: the praise and service of God and neighbor.

Not only do these people menace their own soul's salvation, but they are parasitic bores, and occasions for sin for their fellows.

The measure of our health is this: How well does our body serve us in our mission of restoring all things in Christ? It is true that our bodies are the temples of the Holy Ghost. This means first that our love for the Holy Ghost should take precedence over and regulate our concern for the temple.

Everywhere we find bodies wasted by disease, torn by suffering, bearing witness by holiness and zeal to the fact that the Life within them flows from Christ. Alongside of them, we see busy men of rugged countenance wielding their clubs, bats, and rackets, preserving a body whose sole contribution to God and nature will be the eventual fertilization of its last, undignified, resting-place.

NOVELTY

NOVELTY

It is significant that our moderns have adopted as a salutation the question: "What's new?" The thirst for novelty today is far in excess of normal curiosity. The exclamation, "Let's do something new" is no longer a smiling suggestion. It has become a despairing plea. *The life of the people is spent passing fervently and hopefully from one station to another, dwelling for a moment on each of the latest passions.* "Devotional" literature, proceeding from the monetarily inspired pen and brush of American genius, floods the markets. Yesterday a new soap; today a new song; tomorrow a new foreign policy. A magazine for the new home; a monthly for the new era; a trade journal for a new way of canning beans.

From hats to dresses; from Crosby to Sinatra; from "Forever Amber" to "Peace of Mind"; from urbanism to bio-dynamism; from Winchell to Pegler; from Mandarin lip paint to Magenta; from

up-do to page boy; from morning to night; from
cradle to grave: this is the polytheistic sect of the
New Mysticism.

That the devil looks after his own has rarely been
questioned. Here in America he has outdone himself in generosity. He has furnished us with any
number of ways for peeling potatoes (or avoiding
peeling potatoes), for diagnosing our innards, or
for singing at Mass. Every hamlet has at least five
organizations who school their members in the art
of speaking with the tongues of men and of angels
—without charity. The sounding brass and tinkling
cymbals drawn off from this process supply the raw
ingredient for an equal number of organizations devoted to modern music.

It is possible for anyone who is bored to connect
himself with some corporation devoted to the task
of moving mountains by faith—faith in Yankee
know-how and private enterprise. All of which can
be accomplished—without charity.

Hear the chant of the moderns . . .

"Have you tried my recipe for 'White Death'?
First you take a jigger of brandy, add the juice of

one grapefruit." . . . "This is *the* blouse. It has a sort of decolleté neckline." . . . "Add to this the white of two eggs." "Thrills for the eye and palate." . . . "Gable's back and Garson's got him." . . . "And to relieve the severity there is a diaphanous cloud of wispy lace." . . . "Have you seen 'The Lost Week-end'?" . . . "Back again by popular request." . . . "Toasted nut ice cream." . . . "Bogart is back, Humphrey Bogart (right), and his wife Lauren Bacall (left), stand beside Frances Henderson, New York stage actress." . . . "Oh, wait a minute. It's time for Fibber Magee and Molly."

The United States government spent 2,000,000,-000 dollars to develop the atomic bomb. Every year the American people spend nearly as much to develop atrophy of the mind. More than to any other single factor, the industrial advancement of our nation can be attributed to the ceaseless activity of one hundred million people desperately seeking to escape the necessity of pondering the first five questions in the penny catechism.

Novelty is the quest of fools. Somewhere in-between two notions or three vanities there is a pause. Thank God for that pause! Cling to it! It is the hand of freedom reaching between the bars that hold you prisoner. Weave these pauses together with a strong thread of Christ's Gospels. Hold nylons up to the light of eternity and see how sheer they are! The Hands of Christ and Mary were glorified by work and sacrifice, not by scented soaps. Hold tight to one thought as you would to one spouse. Learn from one spouse the ways of all mankind.

There are no new words. Then let the quiet hear but one Word.

"In the beginning was the Word and the Word was with God, and the Word was God. . . . He was in the world, and the world was made by Him and the world knew Him not. . . ." Because they were all listening to a new Quiz Program.

ADVERTISING

ADVERTISING

THE accompanying cartoon symbolizes the modern institution of advertising. A mannequin is the commercial measure of a man or woman. It isn't the esthetic measure found in the fine arts, nor the moral or virtuous measure found in the saints. The mannequin is what a commercial clothier *thinks* of a potential customer. The mannequin is what the clothes seller wants his customer to look like (or imagines she looks like) so that she will fit (or think she fits) the clothes he has in stock. That is the task that advertising sets out to accomplish: to make the person fit the goods. Thus, in the cartoon, the advertiser (symbolized by the artist) remodels the person to resemble the mannequin.

In every age the artists, poets, dramatists, and actors have been called upon by the leaders of their society to popularize or *put across* in intelligible and understandable form the ideals upon which the society operated. The active ideal of our society has been for some time now individual self-aggrandise-ment, commonly called *bettering oneself*, and tech-nically called *free enterprise*. The leaders of our society, the men who buy and sell things, naturally find this ideal to their liking and employ the genius of our artists, poets, and dramatists to see that the ideal is not permitted to die. The medium they use is called advertising.

Any institution designed to form popular habits and tastes is either the mouthpiece for a religion or a philosophy. If the appeal is to reason, then it is a philosophic movement; if the appeal is to faith, then it is a religious movement. Advertising obvi-ously doesn't appeal to reason. There are no argu-ments over the philosophic validity of an ad. You either *believe* advertisements or you don't. Adver-tising has a mystical appeal—it sings the praises of the new god *Matter*.

The apostles of this new religion are by far the most vigorous, and the most hungry for converts, of any in our time. If a citizen were to suffer the same physical treatment at the hands of another citizen as all of us suffer psychologically at the hands of the advertisers, the act would be punished as criminal. Upon entering a street car or bus, or, if we are so imprudent as to turn on our radio or open a newspaper or magazine, we are suddenly knocked to the ground, a pretty girl rumples our hair and sings crooningly in our ear while a comedian grabs our feet and tickles them; then a sly pickpocket reaches into our wallet and extracts the amount of cash prescribed by the nefarious gang who hires him. Should we develop a defense for this type of assault, the enemy attempts a flank movement. Little Junior pipes up at breakfast that he will not eat any other cereal but a certain anemic sawdust creation with a virile name. The method used in this case is bribery and blackmail. Once you get Junior well in hand (in the right places), you discover to your horror that the next-door neighbor is also a convert to the new mysticism. Your wife mentions that washing dishes has become somewhat of a trial, the spy from next door (not necessarily a member of the party but a follower of the party line) begins to expound about the wonderful new combination ironer and dish-washer now available at the corner swindlers' for only one thousand dollars and ninety-eight cents.

Objectively this is a laughing matter; in reality it is to weep. It is no laughing matter to have the entire artistic genius of the nation urging the people to become solicitous about what they wear and what they eat, when one happens to be dedicated to promoting the ideals and principles of a Man Who said, "Be not solicitous." Using soap is not being solicitous, but using Gleemo, which employs one thousand people to make it and two thousand people to wrap it in cellophane, paint pictures about it, write dramatic skits for it, abstract phrases from the Book of Wisdom to describe it, ship it from coast to coast, sell it, re-sell it, and re-re-sell it . . . that *is* being solicitous. The same goes for all the things we wear or put inside us.

What to do about it? There is more than a hint in the teachings of the Apostles of another age. One of them, Matthew, carefully transcribing the words of His Master, wrote: "Therefore I say to you, do not be anxious for your life, what you shall eat; nor yet for your body, what you shall put on." The sentence preceding this one reads, "You cannot serve God and mammon." The great concern of advertising for what we eat and put on is an *effect*, not a cause. The cause is a mystical worship of mammon.

THE REGULAR GUY

THE REGULAR GUY

EVERY AGE has had its heroic figure. This heroic figure personifies the ideal man of his time. At one time it was the prophet, with flowing beard and flashing eyes. At another, it was the crusader, riding proudly upon his steed, with a cross upon his shield and upon his breast. For short but momentous periods in history, when the tide of virility was at the flood, the ideal man was the saint. These were the radical reformers, Dominic Guzman, Francis of Assisi, moved by the Hand of God. And when religion became man-centered instead of God-centered, there were Calvin, Luther, and Knox, and later Wesley, Joseph Smith, and Brigham Young. At still another time men saw their ideal in the conquistador, and the explorer. Our own fathers remember their boyhood adulation for the frontiersman of the West. And the last of these but one was the man of wealth, the powerful tycoon, the man who built miles of railroads, erected skyscrapers,

dammed lakes, and spanned rivers with never a cal-
loused hand. Today we have the Regular Guy.

The Regular Guy is the man facile in all those
fields that require neither courage nor initiative.
He is the man maidens fancy and wives despise. He
has all the lovable virtues of the child, but none of
the virtues of the man. He is a man of leisure. He
knows how to have a good time, likes to be called
by his first name, dances well. He is charming. He
dresses with studied carelessness. He practices non-
chalance before his mirror. To preserve his gaiety
of manner, which with him is in the nature of a
vocation, he avoids responsibility. He is at home
among women.

The Regular Guy is the hero of the easily satisfied. He satisfies the desire of the girl who wants in
a man a mirror to reflect her own vanity. He satisfies
the desire of the man who wants to remain a gay
young blade—indefinitely. He satisfies the desire
of the layman who expects in his priest nothing
more than a smiling hail-fellow-well-met who goes
around like Pollyanna doing good and clucking his
tongue at evil. He satisfies the doting mother who

would prefer that junior should never grow up. He satisfies the citizen who thinks it fine to be able to call the President of the United States "Harry." He lightens the lives of all those people who choose to think that life is just a bowl of cherries with whipped cream on top.

This mysticism of the Regular Guy perpetuates that very mediocrity in which, our Holy Father warns us, we cannot take refuge. The Church holds up before us day after day in her liturgy, men and women moulded to the likeness of Christ. These saints, while not discarding their childhood virtues, permitted them to be cultivated to a splendid maturity under the persuasion of the Holy Ghost. It is the Incarnation that makes man a twice-noble thing. By implication the Regular Guy denies the effects of the Incarnation. He misleads us into supposing that we can remain in the nursery until the angel of death comes to call. His way is a mockery of the Sacrament of Confirmation that calls us to a virile manhood in the Cause of Christ.

Today it is in those fields where masculine virtue is required that we find things at their worst. Our education lacks a philosophic sense. Philosophy is a masculine field. Politics are corrupt. The forum is for the man. Security is considered the greatest good. Security is for women. Freedom is sought by the very few. Only men can put freedom before security. The family is decaying because mothers and wives are trying to rule in the abdication of the fathers. And it is the Regular Guy who has left the apostolate up to the women.

It is time for all of us to let the grace of Confirmation work in us, and recognize the Regular Guy for what he is—the eternal adolescent.

LUCK

LUCK

A GLANCE at the accompanying illustration might lead the casual reader to expect a tirade on the evils of betting. Such a conclusion would be unjust. It would be unjust simply because it was casual. The isolated act of placing a bet might be something very nice or something very naughty. It is a sign of charity to be able to overlook a little dirt, but a mountain (which is a considerable amount of dirt) is not so easily overlooked. Playing the horses as an individual escapade is of minor importance. For a nation to adopt the institution of gambling as part of its make-up can be a major tragedy. It might mean that the laws of God are losing adherents to the law of averages. It might mean that "Lady Luck" is usurping the title of Providence.

The man and wife of the illustration have decided that "Hayburner, in the third" is a better wager than "Give-us-this-day-our-daily-bread."

This act of personal conversion will be followed by their participating the following afternoon in the corporate act of worship with other members of the faithful.

It is apparent that going to the track is a pilgrimage. The pilgrims, as we know, wear distinctive costumes, and are usually well supplied with devotional literature. The track is the shrine where the miracle has occurred before. Many have borne witness to the beneficence of Lady Luck on the occasion of her various appearances.

In the corporate act of sacrifice the horses are the victims. As in all such sacrifices we find here the characteristic placing of oneself in union with the victim: "I am on Hayburner!"

"They're Off" is the warning cry that communication is about to be made with the deity. Some of the congregation become filled with the spirit, rolling their eyes, twitching, or crying out mightily. Others are tense in a prayerful silence of complete communion. And then, with the roar of many voices, occurs the miracle! Lady Luck pays off!

Gambling cannot be explained apart from religion. The inveterate gambler is filled with a spirit. He is enchanted by the rolling dice, the spinning wheel, the galloping horses, and the turning card. These things have a sacramental significance for him. They are an outward sign of a providence that works invisibly.

Unconsciously, the gambler testifies to man's dependence upon a power greater than himself. When he places his last dollar on the table, his act of surrender to Lady Luck resembles the abandonment of the Christian to God. He gives up all that he possesses so that he may acquire the jewel without price. He abandons himself to the spinning wheel as the saint abandons himself to the towering Cross.

There the resemblance ends. Lady Luck is blind. The providence of God is the merciful concern of an all-powerful and all-loving Father for His children. It is this very difference which gives the gambler his peculiar character. Mercy always presupposes justice. The providence of God has been promised to those who look to the Kingdom of Heaven and its *justice*. The relation between God and those for whom He has a special providence is one of mutual love and mutual justice. This is the kind of mutuality foreign to the system of pari-mutuel. The gambler wants a pay-off with no strings attached. He wants providence without justice.

"I ONLY WORK HERE"

"I ONLY WORK HERE"

As PONTIUS PILATE, procurator of Judea, sentenced The Son of God to death, he washed his hands of the guilt. This is the classic case of passive barbarism. Here we see, at its worst, murder by remote control. Placed as he was in the position of meting out justice in a case for which he had no liking, he stood awkwardly between the irate mob and the quiet scorn of his superiors. His social prestige was threatened; and his power; and his pocketbook. So, he backed out. Had he been alive today, as he looked into the innocent face of the Divine Prisoner, he might have said, "Don't bother me, mister, I only work here." It is with these words that conscience is spurned today.

John Bilge is dismissed from his job without regard for his or his family's welfare. He is told by the personnel manager, "Circumstances necessitate our dispensing with your services." With this pronouncement, the personnel manager, the president, the board of directors, and the stockholders all plunge their hands into the basin. Carefully they *lux* away the guilt of the Bilge family's deprivation.

Mrs. Ajax looks into the mirror. Vanity fails to erase the wrinkles that vanity has produced. The paint is beginning to cake in the crevices. She attributes her waning youth to the demands put upon her by little Junior. She renews her resolution that Junior will not have any brothers or sisters. Then she carefully washes her hands of the lives she intends to deny.

Al McThimble has just discovered that the bank at which he works has recently foreclosed the mortgage on his brother's new home. He has seen foreclosures before. This is the first time that he has seen the resultant misery and hardship in all its details. What is he going to do about it? After all, he only works there! He is going to sit right down and wash his conscience in beer.

Miss Lobhead has noticed that her fiance is becoming more and more amorous. As she applies her "seductive" lip-rouge she sighs wistfully over the fact that he doesn't as yet earn enough money to keep her in the style to which she intends to become accustomed. She adjusts her peek-a-boo neckline, applies a few drops of "Desire" perfume to the prescribed places, and wonders how she can tell him that they must postpone the marriage for at least another year. Before slinking down the stairs to meet him, she carefully washes her hands of her beloved's sins, being careful not to mar the perfection of her nail-job.

Jim McSwindel needs money to play the horses. He pads his expense account lavishly, smiles wisely, and washes his hands.

Never before in history has there been a time of so many injustices with *no one* responsible for them. Very nice people publish filthy literature simply to make an *honest* living. Politicians ruin the country in their desire to spend themselves selflessly for their constituents. Parents work their fingers to the bone in order to make snobs out of their children. Social-minded philanthropists endow institutions to instruct the poor in the art of having fewer anthropoids. Religious schools instruct their students in money-making in the naive assumption that a knowledge of finance is a disposition to virtue.

Perhaps the difficulty of pinning the sin upon any one person is an indication of a corporate guilt. The fact may be that we are all guilty. It is certainly true that we are guilty if we are doing nothing about the social institutions that perpetuate vicious irresponsibility. Our Holy Father has called everyone to an organized apostolate designed to restore a climate in which educated consciences will set the standards. It is safe to say that if we are not *with* this Cause, then, certainly we are against it. That being the case, washing our hands will do no good.

BIGNESS

BIGNESS

MISTER Ten Percent is the biggest thing that ever happened! His empire is the world; his wealth, the wealth of the universe. Diamonds from Africa, wheat from Minnesota, coffee from Brazil, fashions from Paris, tea from India, pictures from Hollywood; all of these have swollen the coffers of the god of Ten Percent. It was he who launched the Queen Mary. He built New York. He created gigantic farms, colossal stockyards, titanic chain stores, seas of soda pop, mountains of tobacco, row upon row of crosses, and the B29.

During his reign, there was but one crime: to be small. It became the law: to be small is to be eaten. The cobbler on the corner, the small shopkeeper, the barber, the tailor, were here yesterday. Where are they now? You will find them tucked away being digested in the warm belly of the Big Store, or permitted a sad existence under the moist thumb of the Huge Monopoly. The small farm—where is that? It is now part of Mister Big's 10,000-acre land-mine. And where is the farmer? He is now working for Mister Big, a small cog in a big machine.

We overhear conversations that go like this:

Daddy smokes BIG cigars. He met a BIG meat man in a BIG restaurant in the BIG city. They have a BIG deal on. There is BIG money involved. He plans to send me to a BIG school so that I can get a BIG job with some BIG concern.

Like the Tenebrae services on Holy Thursday, the tiny lights of small shops and small people are put out one by one, until there is but one light left burning: the light of Mister Big.

Round about this Giant, the apostles of the obvious have spun their shallow mysticism. It is this mysticism which concerns us here, rather than the economics from which it has sprung.

The Christian must constantly struggle to prove this proposition: that the invisible is more important than the visible; that the kingdom not of this world is greater than any kingdom here upon earth.

The spirit is more than the flesh. The unseen reality more than the visible symbol.

The mysticism of Bigness contradicts this proposition. Bigness is quantity, and quantity is visible. QUANTITY has been given primacy over the less tangible but more important QUALITY. This mysticism leads us to place our confidence in physical strength, in large organization, in worldly power. Nazareth, the tiny jewel, the pinpoint concentration of Divine power, has been forgotten. Humility, the weapon of the weak, has been discarded. The quiet prayer is lost in the noise of the world, radio-amplified.

Nowhere can we find men who will say, "Indeed it is true. It is the strength of prayer which is the weapon invincible."

Instead men go about stiff-necked saying, "I represent Amalgamated Soups, Incorporated," or, "this town is too small for me," or, "Stalin sent me," or, "find out what you want, Bub, and then take it."

Nature will tolerate Bigness for just so long. Many centuries before this, the heavy tread of mam-

moths and leviathans had been heard on this planet
After their passing came silence. Silence, unless
one listened closely for the scratching of tiny creatures. These tiny things of wisdom had watched the
giants black and bloody against the sky, strong in
the glory of battle. Later, they had feasted at the
requiem, these tiny things, and had grown strong.

The atom bomb is very small. New York, Lon-
don, or Moscow would make fine targets, but never
Nazareth. Nazareth is too small to bother with.
Nazareth will survive.

PRETENSE

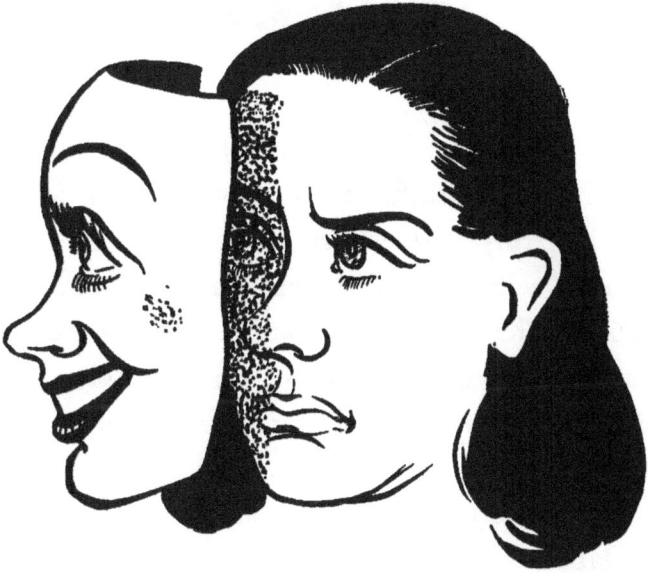

PRETENSE

WHAT a rare treat it is to discover a person without guile! How delightful it is to meet a person whose exterior truly and artlessly reveals his interior! There is something of the actor and the mimic in all of us. This is a talent not without its uses. Today, however, the art of pretense is deliberately culti- vated for use off stage. It has become a mysticism with many an ardent disciple.

The use of clothing for deceit rather than orna- mentation is one of the practices commonly flowing from this new religion. When Joe Snow goes look- ing for a job that pays thirty dollars a week, it is expected that he approach the personnel manager with all the assurance, dignity, and sartorial splen- dor of a man accustomed to an income of ten thou- sand a year. A housewife going downtown to pur- chase a handle for her flatiron is required to dress up as though she were an opera star about to meet her public. A girl of sixteen feels obligated to appear twenty-five. This same sense of obligation returns once she has passed thirty. College undergraduates alternately don masks of brilliant boredom or of boring brilliance. The prevailing mood of the moment is indicated among the males by their choice of ties; among the co-eds by their choice of kerchief or lip-rouge.

This mysticism has its own hierarchy of virtues. For example, righteous indignation is expected of every motorist who is in any way impeded along the way by another motorist. If he is a bus- or taxi-driver, apoplexy is obligatory. It would be improper, however, to unleash this same anger if one heard God blasphemed, or one's neighbor criticized. The recommended emotion under these circumstances varies according to *who* makes the remark. If he is your social equal or inferior, an inscrutable smirk is recommended. If he is your superior, either a hearty laugh or an unqualified affirmation will do the trick.

Further recommendations are these: clergymen and educators must be regular guys, usurers and undertakers must be dignified, cab-drivers and hairdressers must be talkative, commercial men must look prosperous, lawyers must look solemnly intelligent, salesmen must look radiantly intelligent, train conductors and elevator operators must be unintelligible, etc. . . . The roles in which Hollywood has cast the Brooklynite, the Bostonian, and the Texan, are such as to bring tears to the eyes of the stranger who watches a native being dutifully peculiar.

By contrast with others, this mysticism may seem of minor importance. "Appearances don't count for much one way or the other," you may say. "It is what the person himself and God *knows*, that matters."

That isn't entirely true. Catholics have an obligation to bear witness, to make their faith incarnate, to testify before men. A cultivated pretense or affectation makes it difficult for our bodies to express what our minds and hearts contain. If our faces and tongues and hands have been taught to hide our true sentiments beneath conventional deceits, they will not be true to us when we wish to use them sincerely.

A despairing neighbor some day may look to us for a testimony of the Faith which he needs so badly, and we may, by retaining the conventional silence or by showing the conventional embarrassment, leave him to his despair. Another friend may be suffering a great sorrow and need our tears. Instead of telling him about the way of the Cross, we will play an unconvincing Pollyanna dishing out fluff about silver linings. He will go away unconsoled. And there is that last fatal possibility, that when it comes our time to die, in imitation of so many reel-life heroes, our last breath may be wasted asking for a cigarette, instead of the merciful forgiveness of God.

SPEED

E. WHLOCK

SPEED

THE effect of the mysticism Speed is shown in all the activities of the modern man ranging from the casual pilot seated in his supersonic rocket, to the assembly-line worker twitching and chain-smoking after his day's work. Waiting for the next section of a revolving door to come around has become a trying experience. A car or radio that is slow to warm up provides the modern speed demon with the same kind of torture formerly generated by a hair-shirt. Cigarette and chewing-gum makers have put detachable tabs on their packages so that we may not exhaust our patience extracting the contents. A new razor saves us thirty seconds in changing blades, so purchasers beat a path to the counters. Speed has become an end in itself.

Why is it that an era dedicated to the production of labor-saving devices should produce a race of neurotics, unable to relax, and consumed by a sense of urgency? Just to answer that question we have to slow down and relax. The phenomenon of speed is very obvious, especially if you are trying to cross a busy street. The mysticism of Speed can only be seen if we approach it slowly. That is the nature of false religions: the more you embrace them, the less you know about them. You cannot rationalize and enjoy sense-gratification at one and the same time.

Speed satisfies two of man's inner compulsions. The first is a desire to be moved by a great force. The second is the desire to accumulate experiences. When John Smith is traveling along at five miles per hour on foot, he is a very busy man. When Joe Doakes is luxuriating in the delight of speed, he is slothfully reclined on cushions being propelled through space by a powerful machine. Being modern, Joe measures the worth of things by the way they make him *feel*. Joe feels the power of the engine, and because he is a sensate, not a philosophic or religious man, he feels that he, too, is powerful. This is why behind the wheel of a car, despite his usual timidity, he assumes the attitude of Marie Antoinette toward the vile pedestrian.

The modern man is always afraid that he is miss-

ing something. That is because he is inordinately
interested in material things. There are always
enough spiritual goods to go round. Take love, for
instance. My love for Aunt Matilda can increase
day by day, without detracting one iota from my
love for Uncle Fred. A spiritual good can be end-
lessly distributed without being thinned out. But
the modern man is not interested in spiritual goods.
When he is indulging himself in one material thing
he is afraid that he may be missing the delight of another. If he is in New York, he wishes he were in
Chicago. If he is eating spaghetti, he wishes he
were eating oysters. This fanatical desire to accumulate experiences gives him a sense of urgency,
and speed is the outlet for this pent-up emotion.

The mysticism of speed prevents a Christian
from appreciating the wonder of the Present Moment. He is always trying to get away from the
present. Yet the present moment is our point of
contact with God. What we are doing *right now* is
either the source of our happiness or the cause of
our misery, dependent upon whether we accept
God's Will or reject it.

Speed nails a man to the hands of a clock. All day long he is being pulled and twisted by a mechanical monster. If we were to come down from the clock and embrace the cross, we would find that God is a far less difficult task-master than mammon. He only wants us *right now,* not yesterday at 3:15, not tomorrow at eight o'clock.

PROGRESS

PROGRESS

THE law which compels everything that goes up eventually to come down does not have disastrous consequences if the ascent and descent are subject to control, such as in a plane or an elevator. It is only the thing which is up without any means of support that inevitably falls with a thud.

The law of gravity has its counterpart in the spiritual order. Hope which reputedly "springs eternal" causes our spirits to rise. Hope which has some validity will control the rate and height of the ascent of our spirits, and will also, like a well-piloted airliner, bring us back to earth gently when we meet with reverses. Unwarranted optimism, on the other hand, which flings us into an imaginary heaven, will desert us completely after a time, and from our unsupported position in space we will fall like a rocket into the pit of despair. Sarah Dringle believes that every day in every way she is getting better and better. Optimistically looking at the ideal

Sarah of some future date, Miss Dringle ignores her
increasing vanity which will inevitably lead her to
a cranky, fault-finding spinsterhood.

In the light of this reasoning we can see that
much of today's cynicism and despair, instead of
being the contradiction of lighthearted optimism,
is really a result of the latter. Despair is usually the
hang-over from a siege of synthetic hopefulness.

Belief in human progress is a mysticism which
generates unwarranted optimism. Personal or his-
toric experience gives us no justification for believing in inevitable human progress. There is no law
which states that things *must* become better and
better, or that people will become more and more
prosperous, or that governments will become more
and more conformable with human dignity. History
proves the contrary. Both men and civilizations are
subject to disease, senility and death. Every human
institution carries within itself the seed of its own
destruction. Maturity is a prelude to decay. The
path of glory leads but to the grave.

Yet the leaders of our society propagate and
practice a belief in an inevitably bright and joyous

future. Congressman Higelsby knows that an obstinate labor leader is about to clash with an equally obstinate industrialist. The resultant strike will cause a fuel shortage for the entire nation. Yet, in his hometown speech, he speaks in superlative terms of the rosy future ahead. It is implied that all that is needed to assure future beatitude is to keep smiling and believing, and then, "Presto! Chango!" from total chaos will emerge the millennium.

Hope for the future cannot be a tenable position unless it is substantiated by past experience and present virtues. Death cannot be erased with a smile. Unemployment is not relieved by optimism about the future. Wars are not averted by a desire for peace which prompts neither repentance for past sins nor reform of present vices. Hopefulness without foundation is a game of pin-the-tail-on-the-donkey, played blindfolded in a crowded street car. The good that God has in store for men cannot be won like a kewpie-doll at a church bazaar.

When Saint Basil the Great was threatened with confiscation, exile, torture, and death, he replied:

"Is that all? Not one of these things troubles me. From him who owns nothing, no goods can be confiscated. Banishment I cannot know, for everywhere on God's earth I am at home. Torture cannot touch me, for I have no longer a body. Death, however, is welcome to me, for it will bring me more swiftly to God."

Here is an example of Christian optimism, of which the mysticism of progress is a modern caricature. The future *is* inevitably bright for the man who places his hope in the eternal goodness of God. The Christian is assured that in the end everything will turn out all right. Christ made this certain by His Passion and Death. It is the Cross, the same Cross upon which He died, that lifts us up in Christian hope. No other vehicle than this Cross can be trusted to lift our hearts and justify our hopes.

POPULARITY

POPULARITY

OF ALL the impositions placed upon him by his Creator, it is doubtful that any is more odious to Satan than being denied the pleasure of originality. As the new mysticisms haunt the stage for a few brief stanzas and then pass into oblivion, they resemble each other remarkably in that they are all caricatures of the same thing. It is as though a character in Poe, having murdered his spouse, were to seek diversion in painting, only to find that his subjects—human, animal, or pastoral—inevitably assumed the form or visage of the deceased. The mysticism of popularity is, due to the lack of originality of Satan, a caricature of Christianity.

Limelight is to the apostle of the popular what the clear light of grace is to the Christian. It is a sign of election. Many are called, but few are chosen. The chosen few, whose names clutter the tabloids and the air-waves like a strange unending hagiography, epitomize the many who only stand

and wait. These wait along the parade routes, or in queues leading to ticket windows. These are the avid readers of the gossip columnists, parasites who have dedicated their pens to glorifying the new saints of the cinema.

Not all of us can be beatified by the press and canonized by the camera, but in our own humble way we can imitate them. Though our teeth shine not so brilliantly, we can use the same dentifrice (the large economy size). We may lack the wisdom infused by gag-writers, yet we can repeat their clichés until they become part of us: "You ain't kiddin'!" "It's a joke, son!" "That I know!" "That's all, brother!" "Hubba, hubba!"—and similar substitutes for rational conversation.

We of the many who are merely called can preserve our dignity by clutching the tail of a popular kite and hurl our scorn at all those who are less bekited. An insult directed at Ted Williams we can learn to assume as a personal affront. The name of Perry Como we shall defend, if necessary, to the death. Never in our presence may an aspersion be cast upon our secret love.

There is a similarity between the touted productivity of the modern assembly line and the method of producing modern social habits. The factory does not produce many things. It produces the same thing many times. Despite the diversity which characterizes the works of God, the moderns have succeeded in hiding the diversity beneath an assumed handful of types. A pattern which originates in Hollywood is used as a die to stamp out human prototypes all over the country. This leading man and that leading lady will be imaged at every soda fountain and business office in the land. You see inscrutable Robert Mitchums badly in need of a hair cut, smoking cigarettes in every railroad station. Van Johnsons are as thick as flies. Every sandlot has a Joe Di Maggio in the outfield. It has become necessary to unwrap every individual from the role he is playing before you can discover who he actually is.

The chicken and the egg give us a key to this old situation. All eggs look alike because they are sterile. It is not until an egg is fertilized that it becomes a distinct kind of chicken. As long as people choose to be reasonably exact facsimiles of celebrities, their own characters will be sterile. If they choose, however, to become one with Christ, their personalities will mature, and each will develop the unique beauty which makes one child of God so different from another.

SUCCESS

SUCCESS

As IT IS generally used, success is a nice word for something quite nasty. This is most frequently the case when the reference is to financial success or growth in social stature. Success is the thing way out yonder. It is the end that justifies the meanness. It is where the go-getter is going. Success is super-deluxe, A-number-one, free-wheeling PRIDE. Success is the strongest cave-man smirkingly devouring the choicest hunk of meat filched from the common pot.

The whole question of Success is a question of man and his needs. There is nothing a man needs more than a heaven. There is nothing less calculated to supply this need than a heaven on earth. A heaven on earth could never be more than a man-made heaven peopled by unreasonable facsimiles of God. It is just such a perversion as this that men strive for when they strive for success.

The worst sin is wanting to be God. That was

Adam's sin. The man or woman who desires to be praised, to be glorified, to rule, to be obeyed, to be looked up to: that person wants to be God. Desiring these things is expecting that Honor and Glory which is only to be bestowed upon Him Who Is.

Today, the man who possesses just those things necessary for dignified survival is not considered a success, nor is his state generally aspired to. To be in the success class a man must have more than he needs as man: he must have those things befitting an Olympian. He must not merely be clothed for comfort; he must be clothed for display. His car must not merely be adequate; it must be super (for he is superior). Everything he possesses must not be merely enough: it has to be too much.

The victims of this Success mysticism are not only those who are in the success class. Instead it has become a sect by contrast with which the Christians are a small rabid minority. The strangest phenomenon of all is that class who see no incompatibility between the two philosophies. It would seem that to them the sufferings and death of Christ are meaningless peculiarities of His Mission. His worldly failures (they must feel), are in some way attributable to poor planning or His not knowing the right people.

A Christian life, by contrast with that of the success-idealist, is consonant with failure. In a game of dog-eat-dog, a Christian is bound to fail by simply refusing to be a dog. In a society where the "devil can take the hindmost" the Christian must choose the tail end. That is the only charitable thing he can do. When he has chosen or accepted this position, it will be his unspeakable delight to find that there he is truly moving in the best circles, and Christ is there in the midst of them.

MONEY

TIME IS MONEY

MONEY

THE cult of money is the greatest of all idolatries. From the beggar with his pennies to the usurer with his millions, its sweet poison produces spiritual paralysis in all strata of society. *With those who are classed as wage-slaves is treasured this vision: that some morning at ten-thirty the angel of wealth will appear beside their desk (machine, typewriter, counter, etc.) and, breaking their chains, will lead them out into that paradise of pleasure seen so often in the movies. Right by the boss and the time clock they would go, into a world peopled with voluptuaries who all look like movie stars.* Never again would they ride among the rabble or eat among the publicans of the automat! Of course they would be democratic! They would speak kindly with everyone, even with those less fortunate than themselves. Yes, it would be nice to come back for a visit. All this they will have—when they get the money!

It has been pointed out to us that money is the

life blood of the economic system. Analogously, sanctifying grace is the Life Blood of the Mystical Body of Christ. It logically follows, therefore, in a society (traditionally Christian) which has made Economics of primary importance, that money would come to be confused with grace. Having money would be considered as being in the state of grace. Having a dollar is a foretaste of the beatific state of possessing a million dollars. This is not exaggerated simile. It is the only explanation of the current magic of money.

The relation between wealth and work, too, has become extremely distorted. Wealth is supposed to be the result of labor, yet one does not find callouses on the hands of the newly rich. Are these the men with the toil-worn faces? Must they be continually urged to rest, get out in the air more, get a little recreation? Hardly. Any child of this generation could set you right on that score. They will tell you, "There's no money in working for a living. Get yourself a racket! That's the thing to do." This same philosophy phrased with less precision has been adopted, with but rare exception, by our schools. Even the curriculum of our Catholic schools, by contrast with those of a more Christian age, concerns itself more with the thing of mammon (trade and commerce) than with the thing of the guild (the manual arts). Institutions of learning which praise the One True God and at the same time arrange their course of studies to satisfy the demands of mammon have but little time left to consolidate their loyalties. Our God, I am told, is a jealous God.

Then again, the maintenance of one's "station in life" has been used as an excuse for preserving the false class-standards of the bank account. Being engaged in trade or the professions (so-called) does not imply a right to luxuries apparently unbecoming in the poor. Justification for such selfishness is to be found in the cult of money, not in the Gospels.

Christianity demands in such times as these, times of awful impoverishment, that wealth, excessive comfort, or luxury, should hold but small consolation and but little hope. The time has come when voluntary poverty in relation to one's TRUE station in society is the only technique which can mitigate the effects of chaos.

SPORTS

SPORTS

THE business of cultivating childishness has become, in the United States, a multi-million-dollar industry, and the gate receipts are increasing daily by leaps and bounds. The land of make-believe is crowded to capacity, while the real problems of the common good are discussed by an overworked few in half-empty forums. In the street cars and buses, the newspaper readers are more interested in the mock-heroics of Ted Williams than in the grave trials of Secretary Marshall. Each detail of the sports page is perused by the soldiers of Christ while the Encyclicals of the Popes collect dust in the libraries. This is the new mysticism of sports.

Sports and games are the normal occupation of children. Protected, as they must be, against the real problems of life until they are sufficiently mature to cope with them, in their games the children develop various virtues of body and mind useful in later life. As the child passes from adolescence into manhood, the good parent sees to it that the things of the child are dropped to be replaced by the things of the man. For an adult to concern himself daily with mock-problems is a sign of immaturity. In an individual this refusal to grow up is pitiful. For a society of adults to engage their time and energies with games or sports is a curious and tragic phenomenon.

I am not talking about the normal amount of sport that makes for good recreation. The problem here is that of a good thing being monstrously abused.

Batting, throwing, and catching balls is rewarded by an income sometimes in excess of that received by our Chief Executive. The line-plunging talent of a youthful half-back receives the attentive interest of millions of people. In one city, over a half-million dollars is spent in a day, just to watch eighteen men play baseball.

Energies which, if applied to the real problems of society (and God knows we have problems!), might well mean their solution are turned to the business of hitting baseballs, running races, making one's bid, or doing the course in par. The endless details of transporting thousands of men to see a handful of their fellows perform a childish ritual according to an intricate set of rules is accomplished with ease. The problem of feeding starving people is miserably fumbled for lack of enthusiasm, energy or wealth.

Why are men abandoning the forums for the circuses? There is but one explanation. They have ignored or forgotten that each one of us has a specific mission to fulfill, inspired and directed by the Holy Ghost. This calling becomes our responsibility at the reception of Confirmation. The dignity of Christian manhood proceeds from the daily furtherance of this mission. Neglecting this, the man never matures. He remains adolescent.

As men become aware of their mission, we will see fewer scorecards and more missals. The bleachers will be deserted, while additions will be made to the churches and forums. Men will give to the re-Christianization of society the enthusiasm

now extended to the winning of games. Men will
return the bats and balls and clubs to the children,
and take up, in their place, the cross, the sword, and
the plow of manhood.

"ANYTHING FOR
A GAG"

"ANYTHING FOR A GAG"

ONE of the minor virtues is knowing when to laugh and when to be sober. The mean in merriment lies somewhere between the stony-faced Puritan and the laughing hyena. Having a sense of humor is like having a match. If used at the right time, it can evoke a feeling of warmth. In the hands of the careless it may reduce a worthy edifice to a heap of worthless ashes. Ridicule can be an instrument of violence.

A few centuries ago Puritan sobriety lay like a damp fog along the coast of New England. From the coast it was wafted across the country behind the covered wagons of the pioneers. The inevitable reaction against it was not long in coming. The pendulum is now way over on the other side. Now it is the sober and recollected who are the object of witch-hunts. The ducking-stool is reserved for the personality who is quiet and matter of fact. Once men apologized for being drunk. Now we must apologize for being sober. The popular phrase "anything for a gag" generally implies that there is nothing in heaven or on earth so sacred that it cannot acquire higher merit by being used as the object of witticism. This is conceding a degree of virtue to humor far in excess of what it deserves.

The population of this country is fairly well peppered with certain amateur comedians usually referred to by their few friends as "characters." The climate in their vicinity is *toujours gaie*. These are the lads and lassies who can *always* see the funny side of a situation. They sprinkle everything in their path with the dew of ridicule, dedicating all and sundry to the god of Mirth. The more sublime the moment, the greater is their delight in administering a jocular *coup de grace*. The same violence if inflicted with a scowl or sneer would bring down popular wrath about their ears, but because their faces are wreathed in smiles, the act of iconoclasm is regarded as a huge joke.

Take the case of Joe Stevens: he has just awakened with a throbbing headache and a mouthful of fur as a result of a hectic night with the boys. In spite of his mental fog, he is beginning to see for the first time the wastefulness of his life and the vanity of intemperance. He, at the moment, is excellently disposed to the virtue of prudence. Just as he is about to resolve to break his association with the elbow tilters, his phone rings. One of the local "characters" is on the wire. "Hi, Joe! Great morning isn't it. Ha, ha, ha! See if you can screw your head back on and find a hat that will fit it, and I'll meet you down at the bar! I've got a recipe for a pick-me-up that will make you glad it all happened this way! You'll be back at the rail tonight fit as a fiddle! Ha, ha, ha!"

"Ya," says Joe, "I'll see you in an hour."

Or, take the case of J. B. Bloomer. He manages a department store. A moment ago he was approached by one of his elevator operators asking for a raise. The man has been in the store as long as J. B. can remember. He must be nearly sixty years old by now. The injustice of the situation has begun to disturb J. B.'s none too responsive conscience. The fact that a faithful employee after so many years of service should have to come begging for

enough money to live on . . . there must be something seriously wrong somewhere. . . .

His musings are interrupted by the entrance of
Oscar Bright, assistant manager and amateur comedian. "Say, I hear that flannel-feet was in to see you
about a raise! Why, the old goat! He must be rolling in dough. What's he planning to do, buy a new
car? Why, if you give old gran'pa a raise, we'll have
to up the salary of every gold-bricker in the place.
Ha, ha, ha! I almost believe you were falling for his
hearts and flowers routine!"

"Ya," says J. B. sheepishly, "I almost was."

The results of misplaced humor aren't funny.
More people refrain from doing what they know
they should do for fear of being laughed at than
for any other reason. The most compelling ideal
can seem like a foolish dream once it encounters
the vicious tongue of the wise-cracker. Like the sub-
way artist, the gag-man can always crayon a whim-
sical moustache or an absurd pair of spectacles on
his own or another man's vision of greatness.

On the evening of the first Good Friday, some
men retired to their homes in Jerusalem with smiles

of malicious triumph. Others trembled with fear. Some wept with remorse. There were a few, however, who strode into their homes with a jaunty air, slapped their wives on the back, and said, "Sit down dear, and let me tell you the funny thing that happened today. It'll *kill* ya!"

THE LAST MYSTICISM
BUT ONE

THE LAST MYSTICISM
BUT ONE

In the light of Christian tradition it is fairly easy to see the fundamental cause of the growth of these modern mysticisms. It appears that the modern pagan has shut his eyes to reality, at least one of his eyes. He looks at matter, anything he can see, taste, feel, or exploit, but he refuses to look at God, the angels, the demons, eternity, or the human soul. He is dismayed, however, to find that denying these things does not make them any the less real, nor does it quiet his natural longing and curiosity about them. He still hungers for God, while denying His existence.

So, what does he do? He turns from God and spiritual realities, and in desperation attributes the powers proper to spirit to those tangible things about him. Then he builds an entire ritual and religion about his wishful thinking. He tries to assuage the hunger of his soul with material food.

He feeds the spirit with flesh. He wallows in time, and by ignoring death, makes it into a sort of eternity. The rumblings of his stomach he regards as a kind of sacred compulsion.

If these mystical beliefs were merely the odd ideas of a few peculiar people, they would not deserve so lengthy a consideration. The fact of the matter is that they have been made incarnate in stone, cement, steel, paper, glass, film, and above all, in human organization. The business of keeping these myths alive employs thousands of people every day from nine to five. Just consider for a moment the revolutionary consequences if the idols of bigness, progress, glamour, sports, success, money, and security were destroyed! How many of our modern commercial institutions could survive such a return to rationality? Suppose the manufacture of goods was limited to those things that are necessary to dispose men to virtue? Can you imagine anything more revolutionary than that? Yet a restoration of all things to Christ implies just such revolutionary reforms as that. To restore each of these creatures to its proper Christian context is part of the task to which the lay-apostolate of our times is dedicated.

Perhaps we may not see any nation-wide adoption of Christian norms in our time. If we do not, then we shall be witness to the last but one of all material idolatries. The multiple gods will all be gathered together in one fold, and we shall have a material monotheism, the God-State. The agitators of the extreme right and those of the extreme left have already gone far toward incorporating these mystical beliefs into a collective pattern. Every yearning of the human heart, these apostles assure us, will be satisfied by an omnipotent State. Man will find his beatitude in the mass, rather than in the Mass.

Every man who persists in following the material myths is contributing to the building of an eventual God-State. This, in spite of what his views may be about totalitarianism and human freedom. There is a half truth in the Marxian doctrine of economic determinism. It is true that mankind, *without God,* does tend in a certain inevitable direction. The tendency is toward the homogeneous slime from which he was created. A not inapt analogy of the totalitarian state.

Finally, there is a point to which I know I have not given enough stress. It is this: the life of a Catholic is a life of faith. We have the true and only Mysticism. As a result of the Incarnation of Christ and His Death and Resurrection, all matter has taken on a new glory. The universe has been redeemed. Life and creatures have taken on a meaning which can only be perceived through the eyes of faith. Consequently, we must have the greatest compassion upon the modern mystics. It is because they lack the Faith which gives a joyful meaning to life, that they have invented this idolatry. It is certain that if we were to manifest the true Faith as tangibly as they bear witness to their idols, if we were to found Christian institutions, workshops, farm communities, houses of hospitality, and the like, then it would not be long before there would be but one Mysticism, and that the true one.

For lack of bread the moderns are living on cake. They have asked us for bread, and we have given them a stony stare. Let us build a house of bread, a new Bethlehem, in which we shall have the bread of Life, and then the pagans can come and eat with us.